CODE RED
APRIL 14, 1912
Nightmare on the *Titanic*

by William Caper

Consultant: Paul F. Johnston
Washington, D.C.

BEARPORT

New York, New York

Credits

Cover and Title Page, © Max Dannenbaum/The Image Bank/Getty Images; 3, © Mary Evans Picture Library/Alamy; 4-5, © Topham/The Image Works; 6, © Mary Evans Picture Library/Alamy; 8, Courtesy Library of Congress Prints and Photographs Division; 9, © Underwood & Underwood/CORBIS; 10, © The Granger Collection, New York; 11, © Titanic Historical Society; 12, © Father Browne Collection c/o Davison & Associates; 13, © National Geographic Society; 14, © The Mariners' Museum, Newport News, VA; 15, © Hulton Archive/Getty Images/Newscom.com; 16, © Willy Stöwer/ullstein bild /The Granger Collection, New York; 17, © POPPERFOTO/Alamy; 18, Courtesy National Archives; 19, © The Granger Collection, New York; 20, © Hulton-Deutsch Collection/CORBIS; 21, © Mary Evans Picture Library/Alamy; 22, Courtesy Library of Congress Prints and Photographs Division; 23, © Hulton Archive/Getty Images/Newscom.com; 24, Courtesy U.S. Coast Guard; 25, Courtesy U.S. Coast Guard's International Ice Patrol; 26, Courtesy of the Smithsonian Institution, NMAH/Transportation; 27, © Woods Hole Oceanographic Institute; 28T, © POPPERFOTO/Alamy; 28B, © The Mariners' Museum, Newport News, VA; 29TL, © Titanic Historical Society; 29TR, © The Granger Collection, New York; 29B, Courtesy Library of Congress Prints and Photographs Division; 30, © Bettmann/CORBIS; 31, © Mary Evans Picture Library/Alamy.

Publisher: Kenn Goin
Project Editor: Lisa Wiseman
Creative Director: Spencer Brinker
Photo Researcher: Marty Levick
Design: Dawn Beard Creative

Library of Congress Cataloging-in-Publication Data

Caper, William.
   Nightmare on the Titanic / by William Caper.
      p. cm. — (Code red)
   Includes bibliographical references and index.
   ISBN-13: 978-1-59716-362-0 (lib. bdg.)
   ISBN-10: 1-59716-362-7 (lib. bdg.)
   1. Titanic (Steamship) —Juvenile literature. 2. Shipwrecks—North Atlantic Ocean—Juvenile literature. I. Title.

   G530.T6C35 2007
   910.9163'4—dc22

                                        2006028425

For more information, write to Bearport Publishing Company, Inc., 101 Fifth Avenue, Suite 6R, New York, New York 10003. Printed in the United States of America.

10 9 8 7 6 5 4 3 2

Contents

Iceberg Right Ahead!

On the night of April 14, 1912, the *Titanic* was slicing through the cold waters of the Atlantic Ocean. The weather was clear. The sea was calm. The ship was less than three days away from New York City.

At 11:40 P.M., one of the **lookouts** saw something in the water. "**Iceberg** right ahead!" he warned the **bridge**.

The *Titanic* had four smokestacks. However, only three were real. The one closest to the stern, or the back of the ship, was fake. It was added to improve the ship's appearance.

First Officer William Murdoch gave the order to steer left. It was too late, though. The boat scraped against the iceberg. To the people on the bridge, there seemed to be no damage.

However, under the water the iceberg had ripped open the *Titanic*'s **starboard** side. Water started pouring into the ship.

"We've struck an iceberg—a big one—but there's no danger."

—Harvey Collyer, a passenger, to his wife, Charlotte

The *Titanic* had received a warning about icebergs in its path. However, the captain did not post extra lookouts or slow down the ship. It is believed that he thought the *Titanic* could stay clear of the ice.

What Was That?

The *Titanic* shook softly for about ten seconds as it scraped against the iceberg. Many people barely felt the shaking at all. Some passengers who were asleep did not even wake up. Others had no idea what had happened.

This iceberg is located in the North Atlantic Ocean near the one that the *Titanic* hit. A large part of the iceberg is hidden underwater.

The *Titanic* was built to withstand a head-on collision. Its designers did not think an iceberg could damage the sides of the ship so badly.

Thomas Andrews, the head designer of the *Titanic*, and Captain Edward J. Smith inspected the ship. Much to their surprise, they found serious damage below the **waterline**. A lot of water had already poured into the ship. Andrews told the captain that the *Titanic* was going to sink.

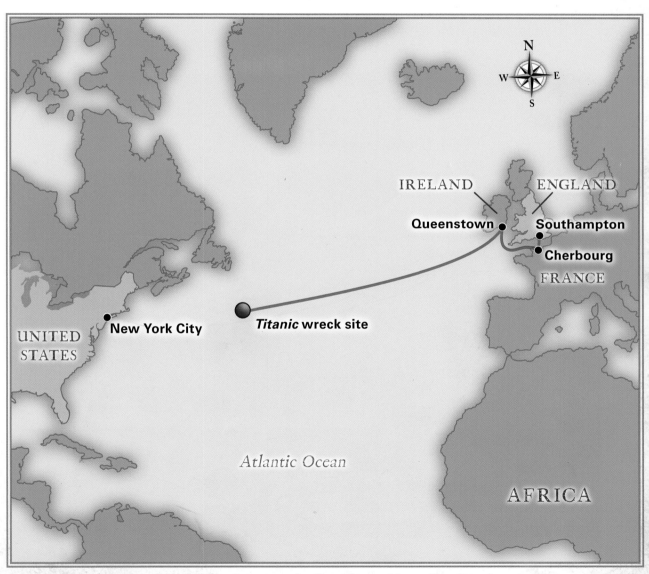

The *Titanic* started its journey in Southampton, England. It made stops at Cherbourg, France, and Queenstown, Ireland. The ship hit an iceberg about 950 miles (1,529 km) from its destination, New York City.

The World's Biggest Boat

In the early 1900s, huge **ocean liners** allowed people to travel the world by sea. The *Titanic* was the largest ocean liner of its time. Built by the White Star Line, it was 882 feet (269 m) long, about the length of three football fields. It reached a height of 175 feet (53 m).

The *Titanic* had three huge propellers. The propellers were so large that they towered over the workmen in the shipyard.

The *Titanic* was more than the world's biggest ship. At the time, it was the largest moving object ever built.

The *Titanic* was on its first trip. It carried more than 2,200 people. Many of the passengers, such as John Jacob Astor, were rich and famous. The *Titanic* offered them many **luxuries**. It had electric lights in every room and fancy dining halls. It also had a heated swimming pool.

Only the wealthiest passengers were allowed to use this elegant room on the *Titanic*.

The Safest Ship

It was not just the *Titanic*'s size that made it unusual. Many people thought it was **unsinkable**.

The bottom of the **hull** was made up of two layers of steel. Many ships had only one layer. If the bottom of the hull were damaged, the second layer would help stop the ship from flooding.

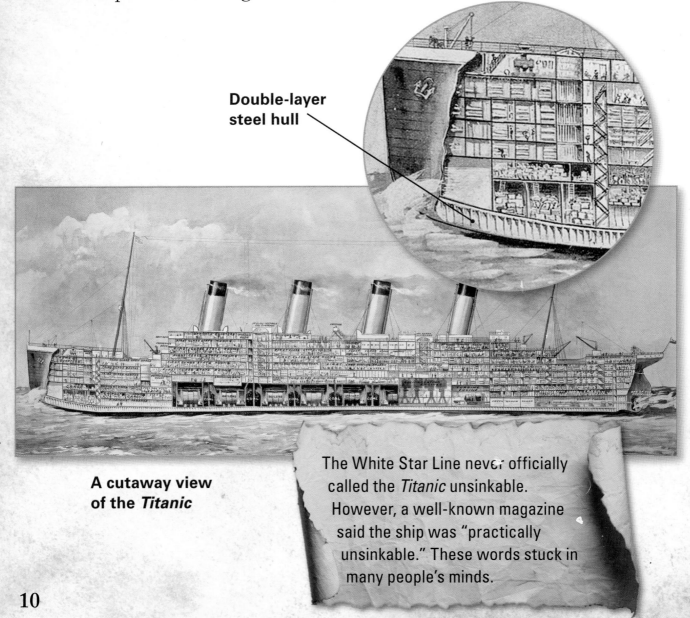

Double-layer steel hull

A cutaway view of the *Titanic*

The White Star Line never officially called the *Titanic* unsinkable. However, a well-known magazine said the ship was "practically unsinkable." These words stuck in many people's minds.

The *Titanic*'s hull had 16 compartments that were separated by special **bulkheads** with **watertight** doors. If water got into a compartment, the bulkheads would stop it from reaching other parts of the boat. Even if two of these compartments flooded, the *Titanic* could still stay afloat.

The doors between the *Titanic*'s 16 compartments could be closed from the bridge at the touch of a button.

" It never entered our heads . . . that a magnificent ship like the *Titanic* could sink."
–Kornelia Andrews, a *Titanic* passenger

Help!

After the *Titanic* hit the iceberg, **telegraph** operators sent out calls for help. One ship, the *Carpathia*, was about 58 miles (93 km) away. It turned around, but even at top speed it would take about four hours to reach the *Titanic*.

Harold Bride, one of the *Titanic*'s two telegraph operators, in the ship's telegraph room

The *Titanic*'s telegraph operators used both SOS and CQD as distress calls. *CQ* stood for "Seek You." The *D* stood for danger or distress.

Lights from a closer ship, the *Californian*, could be dimly seen in the distance. It had stopped for the night because it was surrounded by ice. The *Titanic* fired **distress** rockets into the sky to signal trouble. However, the *Californian* didn't realize the *Titanic* needed help right away. The ship didn't arrive until the morning.

This New York City telegraph operator received word of the *Titanic* disaster from other ships at sea.

"Come at once. We have struck a berg. It's a CQD."

–John Phillips, a *Titanic* telegraph operator, in a message to the *Carpathia*

Women and Children First

By 12:30 A.M., most of the passengers on the *Titanic* were awake. The crew tried to get them into lifeboats on the **port** side of the ship. However, some people refused to leave. They believed the *Titanic* would not sink. They felt safer on the big ship than in the tiny boats.

This picture shows what it might have been like to be on the *Titanic* as passengers prepared to get into the lifeboats.

The *Titanic* was designed to carry 32 lifeboats. However, it had only 20 on board.

Even if people had wanted to leave the ship, many would not have been able to. There were not enough lifeboats. To make matters worse, the crew let many of the lifeboats leave the ship only half full. They did not know how badly the ship had been damaged.

Women and children were put in lifeboats first. Many of the men watched as their families escaped the sinking ship.

Some crew members believed that full lifeboats could not be safely lowered into the water.

Down with the Ship

As more water flowed into the *Titanic*, her **bow** dipped deeper into the sea. Soon, the back of the mighty ship lifted out of the water. It pointed straight up in the air as it sank.

An artist's view of what the *Titanic* may have looked like while sinking.

" She slid slowly forwards through the water . . . The sea closed over her and we had seen the last of the beautiful ship. "

–Lawrence Beesley, a passenger on the *Titanic*

16

While the ship slid below the water, many people were still on board. Some jumped into the freezing ocean, trying to reach a lifeboat. Others stayed on the ship until the very end.

The *Titanic* had a band that played music for passengers every evening. As the boat sank, the band kept playing. The musicians went down with the ship.

The *Titanic* sank at 2:20 A.M. on April 15, 1912. It took the ship only 2 hours and 40 minutes to sink after it hit the iceberg.

Rescue at Sea

Though the people in the lifeboats had escaped, they were still in danger. Many of them had gotten wet. The night air was very cold. They could die from **exposure**.

Around them, they could hear the cries of people in the icy water. Some people in the lifeboats refused to help them. They feared they would fall into the water, too.

Titanic survivors make their way to the *Carpathia*.

" We just rowed about until dawn when we caught sight of the port light of the *Carpathia*, and knew that we were saved."

–Dr. Washington Dodge, a *Titanic* survivor

At about 4:00 A.M., the *Carpathia* finally arrived. The people in the lifeboats knew that they would be saved.

The *Californian* did not arrive until more than four hours later. By then, the *Carpathia* had already picked up the survivors. In all, about 705 people lived. More than 1,500 people died.

Aboard the *Carpathia*, *Titanic* survivors were finally out of danger.

One of the last *Titanic* survivors, Lillian Gertrud Asplund, died on May 6, 2006. She was five years old when her family sailed on the *Titanic*.

How Could It Happen?

The loss of the *Titanic* and so many lives shocked the world. People wanted to know how this great ship could have sunk.

The U.S. Senate held an **inquiry** to learn about what happened. More than 80 people, including passengers and crew members, spoke at this hearing.

The loss of the *Titanic* was big news.

The inquiry revealed important facts about the *Titanic*. For example, the watertight doors had closed as they were supposed to. However, the bulkheads were not high enough. Even with the doors closed, water was able to get into compartments from above. As the *Titanic*'s bow dipped into the sea, more water flowed into the boat, flooding the other compartments.

White Star Line managing director J. Bruce Ismay (the man with his hand on his chin) being questioned at the U.S. Senate inquiry

At the U.S. Senate inquiry, Second Officer Charles Lightoller was questioned for three days regarding the sinking of the *Titanic*.

What If?

Many mistakes led to the loss of the *Titanic*. What would have happened if just a few things had been different?

Some people think the ship might not have sunk if the watertight bulkheads had been one **deck** higher. Others feel the *Titanic* might not have gone down had it had double hulls on its sides, too.

The *Titanic*'s hull had two layers of steel on the bottom, but not on the sides. The ship could suffer serious damage if its sides were hit.

Most agree that more lives could have been saved if there had been enough lifeboats on board. More people would also have lived if the crew had fully-loaded the lifeboats with passengers. Perhaps the biggest mistake the crew and passengers made, however, was thinking that the *Titanic* was unsinkable.

Lifeboats on the *Titanic*

In 1912, ships often did not slow down when they entered areas where there was ice. At this time, people did not know how badly an iceberg could damage a ship.

Changes at Sea

After the *Titanic* sank, new safety rules were put in place. Ships had to carry enough lifeboats for everyone on board. Boats that held at least 50 passengers had to have telegraph equipment that was on day and night.

This is one of the early ships used by the International Ice Patrol to find and track icebergs.

"One had known, full well, and for many years, the ever-present possibility of such a disaster.**"**

–Second Officer Charles Lightoller, speaking at a British inquiry into the disaster

The path of boats sailing in the Atlantic Ocean was moved 60 miles (97 km) south to avoid icy areas. If the ships did enter an icy area, they had to slow down.

In 1914, the International Ice Patrol was started. This group finds and tracks icebergs in the North Atlantic Ocean. It also warns ships about icebergs that are near them.

Today, the International Ice Patrol does much of its work by aircraft.

Currently, 17 countries are part of the International Ice Patrol, a U.S. Coast Guard group.

Finding the *Titanic*

For many years, no one could locate the *Titanic*. In 1985, Robert Ballard, a scientist and ocean explorer, led a new team to search the ocean floor.

Finally, after two months, they found the wreck. It was about 400 miles (644 km) east of Newfoundland, Canada. The ship lay in three large and many smaller pieces, beneath about 12,500 feet (3,810 m) of water. Since 1985, about 5,500 **artifacts** have been recovered and many more have been found in the wreck.

A life vest from the *Titanic*

Today, the story of the *Titanic* still amazes people. It is a tale of both **progress** and terrible loss. This mighty ship has become a symbol of the great things people can do, and the huge mistakes they can make.

The bow of the *Titanic* lies at the bottom of the ocean.

It takes a **submarine** more than two hours to reach the wreck of the *Titanic* from the ocean surface.

Many people played an important role in the events connected to the *Titanic* disaster. Here are five of them.

Edward J. Smith **was the captain of the *Titanic*.**

- Went down with his ship, leaving many unanswered questions about the *Titanic*'s sinking
- Respected by many people, even after the disaster
- Honored by a large statue in Lichfield, England

Charles Lightoller **was the highest-ranking crew member of the *Titanic* to survive.**

- Was one of the officers in charge of loading passengers into lifeboats
- Stayed at his post until the ship started going down, then jumped into the ocean and was able to reach a lifeboat
- Years later, during World War II (1939–1945), used his own boat to rescue 130 soldiers who were trapped on a beach

Harold Bride and **John Phillips** were the *Titanic*'s telegraph operators. They sent many messages asking for help.

- Jumped into the water and were picked up by a lifeboat
- Phillips died from exposure; Bride survived and was rescued by the *Carpathia*
- Once on board the *Carpathia*, Bride sent telegraph messages for survivors to their friends and families

Molly Brown became one of the *Titanic*'s most famous survivors.

- Was so busy helping others that she almost didn't get into a lifeboat; was dropped into a boat as it was being lowered by two men
- Helped row her lifeboat, argued with the person in charge because he would not go back to help others, and gave some of her clothes to other people
- Became known as the "Unsinkable" Molly Brown
- Ran for Congress, and was the subject of a Broadway musical and a movie

Glossary

artifacts (ART-uh-*fakts*) objects of historical interest that were made by people

bow (BOU) the front part of a ship

bridge (BRIJ) a platform above and across the deck of a ship, from which the ship is controlled

bulkheads (BUHLK-hedz) walls separating compartments on a ship

deck (DEK) platform that forms the floor of a boat or ship

distress (diss-TRESS) a condition of danger or desperate need

exposure (ek-SPOH-zhur) the effect that very bad weather has on someone over a period of time

first officer (FURST OF-uh-sur) crew member of a ship who is directly below the captain in rank

hull (HUHL) the frame of a ship

iceberg (EYESS-*berg*) a large floating mass of ice in the ocean

inquiry (in-KWYE-ree) a search for truth or knowledge; a careful examination

lookouts (LUK-*outs*) people who keep watch

luxuries (LUHK-shuh-reez) things that add pleasure or comfort to a person's life, but are not really necessary

ocean liners (OH-shuhn LINE-erz) large ships that carry passengers across the ocean

port (PORT) the left side of a ship

progress (PROG-ruhss) to move forward; improve

starboard (STAR-burd) the right side of a ship

submarine (SUHB-muh-reen) a ship that can travel below water as well as on the surface

telegraph (TEL-uh-*graf*) an electric device for sending and receiving messages

unsinkable (uhn-SINGK-uh-buhl) not able to be sunk; able to stay afloat no matter what happens

waterline (WAW-tur-*line*) a line on the outside of a ship that matches the water's surface when the ship floats evenly

watertight (WAW-tur-*tite*) made so that water cannot get in or get out

Bibliography

Butler, Daniel Allen. *"Unsinkable": The Full Story of RMS* Titanic. Cambridge, MA: Da Capo Press (1998).

Cox, Stephen. *The* Titanic *Story: Hard Choices, Dangerous Decisions.* Peru, IL: Open Court (1999).

Eaton, John P., and Charles A. Haas. Titanic*: Destination Disaster.* New York: W. W. Norton (1987).

Lord, Walter. *A Night to Remember.* New York: Bantam Books (1997).

Merideth, Lee W. *1912 Facts About the* Titanic. Sunnyvale, CA: Rocklin Press (2003).

Read More

Ballard, Robert D. *Exploring the* Titanic. New York: Scholastic (1993).

Conklin, Thomas. *The* Titanic *Sinks!* New York: Random House (1997).

Marschall, Ken, and Hugh Brewster. *Inside the* Titanic. Boston: Little, Brown (1997).

Sloan, Frank. Titanic. New York: Franklin Watts (1987).

Learn More Online

To learn more about the *Titanic*, visit **www.bearportpublishing.com/CodeRed**

Index

About the Author

William Caper has written books about history, science, film, and many other topics. He lives in San Francisco, with his wife, Erin, and their dog, Face.